SCHOLASTIC

D1648726

Managing the
Digital
Classroom

Adam Hyman

Includes a CD with *customizable templates!*

Dozens of Awesome Teacher-Tested Ideas That Help You Manage and Make the Most of Every Digital Tool in Your Classroom

New York • Toronto • London • Auckland • Sydney
Mexico City • New Delhi • Hong Kong • Buenos Aires

Teaching *Resources*

Editor: Maria L. Chang

Cover design by Scott Davis

Interior design by Holly Grundon

SMART Notebook templates design by Jason Robinson

ISBN: 978-0-545-50484-3

Text copyright © 2014 by Adam Hyman

Notebook templates copyright © 2014 by Scholastic Inc.

1 2 3 4 5 6 7 8 9 10   40   20 19 18 17 16 15 14

TABLE OF CONTENTS

PAGE 4 Introduction

PAGE 8 CHAPTER 1:
Setting Up a Technology-Rich Classroom

PAGE 13 CHAPTER 2:
Making the Most of Your Interactive Whiteboard

PAGE 40 CHAPTER 3:
Using Document Cameras to Enhance Learning

PAGE 46 CHAPTER 4:
The Flipped Classroom—What You Need to Know

PAGE 54 CHAPTER 5:
Mobile Learning With Mobile Devices and Tablets

PAGE 62 CHAPTER 6:
Communicating and Collaborating in the Digital World

PAGE 70 CHAPTER 7:
Exploring Social Media

PAGE 76 Bibliography

Introduction

Enter any classroom these days, and you'll be hard pressed not to find some evidence of technology, whether it's one or two computers tucked in a corner of the room or a large interactive whiteboard front and center. What we consider "technology" has changed in the last few decades. In the past, technology may have consisted of a tape recorder, an overhead projector, a laser disk player, or even a slide projector that seemed typical of junior high science classes. Obviously, today's technology tools—which include interactive whiteboards, document cameras, laptops, webcams, tablets, and smartphones—are a lot more sophisticated. As a result, they can feel overwhelming and may even hinder our teaching if we don't understand how to utilize them effectively in the classroom.

The fact of the matter is that technology will continue to shape our classrooms and the way we instruct our students both now and in the future. Today, technology permeates nearly every facet of our lives, including education. It is even woven into the Common Core State Standards. In describing the capabilities of students who meet the standards, the introduction to the English Language Arts Standards states: "Students employ technology thoughtfully to enhance their reading, writing, speaking, listening, and language use. They tailor their searches online to acquire useful information efficiently, and they integrate what they learn using technology with what they learn offline. They are familiar with the strengths and limitations of various technological tools and mediums and can select and use those best suited

to their communication goals." One of the fourth-grade writing standards, for example, expects students to "use technology, including the Internet, to produce and publish writing as well as to interact and collaborate with others; demonstrate sufficient command of keyboarding skills to type a minimum of one page in a single sitting" (W.4.6). Even in first grade, students should "use a variety of digital tools to produce and publish writing" (W.1.6). Educators must therefore give the use of technology a lot of thought when creating engaging lessons for today's student.

There are many opportunities to introduce and use technology effectively in your teaching. Yet, for various reasons, not all teachers feel comfortable incorporating technology into their lessons. Some worry that lessons they plan for the interactive whiteboard may not work the way they had originally intended—and let's face it, that does happen occasionally. Even tech-savvy teachers may not always feel comfortable falling back on a lesson that doesn't use technology when the computer freezes up or a file fails to open.

What we need to understand is that today's students are very adept at technology simply by virtue of being born in the technological age. Take my four-year-old daughter, for instance. She instinctively learned on her own how to use my iPad and smartphone, the microwave oven, and even the TV remote control. She knows how to manipulate the mouse to click on an icon and how to use the touchpad on my laptop. Her hand-eye coordination in moving the pointer across the screen is amazingly accurate. She even knows some computer-related jargon, such as *download*, *open*, and *online*. The point here is that students naturally gravitate toward the use of technology, preferring to use technology for independent work, group work, and any type of work you need them to do. According to a 2012 survey by CDW-G, a provider of technology products and services, 69 percent of high school students said that they wanted more technology in their classrooms. In response, the survey also found educators are shifting away from the old lecture-style approach to lessons and toward a more balanced learning approach by relying on and using more technology tools, such as laptops, tablets, and even smartphones. Classroom technology is rapidly becoming the fast track to increasing student engagement and bringing lessons to life in ways that were previously unimaginable. My advice is to incorporate it, use it, and embrace it.

One of the most effective ways to use technology in the classroom is in small groups, especially for differentiated target groups. This can be done in numerous ways. For example, immediately after a mini lesson, you might bring your target students (no more than five) to the interactive whiteboard to work directly with you. You could do a quick review and assess whether students in the target group understood the lesson and perhaps assign them additional interactive, hands-on practice on the board. This helps ensure that those students who need extra attention or remediation can grasp key concepts and master the skills expected of them. You could also weave technology into small-group projects to give new life and purpose to the work. The trick is to be creative with how you design a project that incorporates technology and meets the standards.

Used correctly, technology invites teachers to become more innovative with their lessons and could even help them run their classrooms more efficiently. Consider these questions when thinking about how you integrate technology into your classroom:

- ✿ Do you use technology in the classroom at all? If so, to what degree?
- ✿ Do you feel comfortable using technology to enhance lessons?
- ✿ How much technology integration do you feel is necessary?
- ✿ Is there a point at which technology becomes too much of a distraction?
- ✿ How can you incorporate the new technology tools for teaching to make your life as an educator easier and more creative, and your instruction more focused for your students?

Many teachers feel unsupported in implementing technology successfully in their own classroom. With so many options available, some don't know where to begin. Occasionally, teachers try new things and may even be eager to do so, but the process may become so haphazard that many quit before giving it a real chance. With this book, I hope to help you tackle these three main areas of concern:

(1) How can you integrate technology effectively to create a more powerful learning environment?

(2) How can you use technology to help you with classroom and time management?

(3) How can you manage technology itself—from connecting your various tools and making them work together seamlessly to troubleshooting, maintenance, and just plain-old keeping up with the speed at which technology changes?

This book is written not just for the rookie teacher but also for the veteran teacher who wants to meet the needs of today's tech-savvy students. In this book, you will have access to some of my most popular digital classroom ideas and strategies—all updated and tweaked to be in sync with today's accessible technology and social media. These ideas will help promote engagement, differentiation, communication, exploration, student-to-student collaboration, and student-to-teacher collaboration, as well as foster creativity and imagination in all grade levels.

We'll start by looking at how to design your 21st-century classroom around the technology that you currently have (and could potentially have down the road). Then we'll focus on how to begin using technology on a day-to-day basis for both classroom management and for instruction. Along the way, I'll provide tips on what to do when the technology fails, compare the pros and cons of various technologies, offer ready-to-use lesson ideas, and more.

It's important to note that with most things these days, technology becomes obsolete rather quickly, changing faster than most of us can keep up with. The objective here is to take in technology fully and accept your role as a 21st-century teacher—one who uses conventional styles of teaching with a technological eye toward change and who can ultimately morph into a tech-savvy hybrid educator as time moves forward. And even if you're still not completely comfortable with technology in your classroom, your students could most certainly help you, and if you play to their strengths, you'll find that they can really surprise you. Enjoy the ride!

CHAPTER 1:

SETTING UP A

Technology-Rich Classroom

I've been in education since 1998, first as a classroom teacher in the fifth and sixth grades, then as a technology teacher and data specialist since 2006. It wasn't until I became my school's technology teacher and received my second Master's in School Building Leadership and Technology, however, that I understood the potential technology has, not just for a school as a whole, but for individual classrooms as well. When considering the classroom management software to help me monitor what students are doing on their computers and laptops, the use of interactive timers and clocks on my SMART Board, and fully interactive lessons that motivate students to participate more, I became very aware of some tactics that I needed to implement in order to improve students' learning experience in my Media Center lab.

When I began integrating technology—starting with the interactive whiteboard—in various areas of the curriculum, I noticed a sudden increase in student engagement. Naturally, as I used more and more technology and expanded my repertoire, I quickly saw that a lot of what I was doing in my technology lab resulted in higher-level thinking skills in my students. It just seemed very logical to supplement traditional paper-and-pencil work with newer, more modern ways of learning and working through technology. So, how do you set up your classroom to integrate the various technology tools available in education today?

Classroom Design With Technology Integration

The layout and design of a classroom directly impact how students learn. There is no question that your classroom environment is the starting point to everything educational, and a 21st-century classroom design is no exception.

If anything, a 21st-century classroom design is even more intricate, and additional thought needs to go into how the classroom functions as a whole. If your classroom is rich in technology use, there are a number of things that need to be considered in order to organize and utilize your equipment in an efficient and practical manner.

To start, look at your classroom from multiple vantage points and notice where the technology is. Do you have desktop stations or a laptop cart? Do you have a class set of iPads or tablets? Where are they located, and where do students go to use them? These are some of the questions to ask yourself when creating (or recreating) your technology-rich classroom environment because, after all, if you have the technology in your classroom, you're going to want to use it effectively and efficiently. There's no use in having an interactive whiteboard in an area of the classroom that isn't conducive for learning. There should be plenty of space to move around and to allow student access to all the various pieces of equipment.

Consider drawing your classroom's layout on paper to get a better understanding of what your classroom looks like and how the floor plan allows for technology integration. Planning it out now will give you a different perspective of what your classroom looks like and how it functions and will give you an idea of how to rearrange it for comfort and ease of mobility later on.

I firmly believe that a purposeful classroom design and layout are key to a successful school day. If the design and layout of your classroom is not conducive to learning and moving about, it's going to make everything else more difficult to do and will ultimately take away from the flow of your day. Particularly when technology plays an important role in your everyday routine, you'll need to pay special attention to how your students and instruction move from one area of your classroom to the next.

The Interactive Whiteboard as the Centerpiece

When designing your room around technology, start with the biggest piece of equipment. In most cases, that would be the interactive whiteboard. Ideally, it would be great if you could discuss with your principal, custodian, and even the vendor/installer the best possible location for the interactive whiteboard before it is mounted on your wall. This way, you don't have to flip-flop your entire classroom and shuffle all your furniture around just to accommodate a new board. However, many teachers may not have a say in the matter so they'll just have to adjust and possibly compromise on a location for the board, perhaps simply because of where the electrical outlets are located in the classroom.

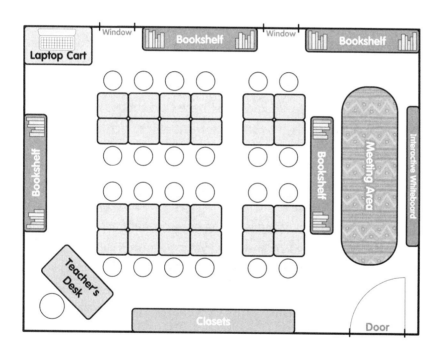

QUICK TECH TIP

Use your SMART Board to help you design your classroom. Create a rough layout design by using the Shapes tool, which can help you manipulate the layout and determine what works best. It will also get you to think about potential problems and visually open up different ways your room can flow.

If, however, you are still waiting for an interactive board to be installed in your classroom, take a look around the room and think about the most conducive location for the board. Look for outlets along the wall. How many do you have? Are there enough to support all the electrical wiring needed to run your board, computer, projector, and/or document camera? Will you need a surge protector and extension cord to accommodate everything if there aren't enough outlets? If the board is going on a wall opposite a bank of windows, will glare be an issue? These are things you'll have to pay attention to prior to the installation. If possible, avoid having an IWB installed in the corner of a classroom, unless you really don't have any other options. The corner of a room will not only limit the space that you have to work, but it also limits the area that your students will have to view and access the board during a whole-class interactive lesson.

Another thing to think about is where your students will sit during an interactive whiteboard lesson. Is there enough room in front of and around the board to house all your students? Will everybody be able to see clearly from where they're sitting? And while your students are sitting in front of the board, how will they come up to the board to interact with it? You wouldn't want to have students sit so close to the board that there's no room for you and at least one other student to stand in front of it to actually interact and use it.

I strongly recommend making the interactive whiteboard the focal point of the classroom and building the learning environment around the board itself. You might want to design and build your classroom library around the meeting area in front of the board so that you have a well-defined space for your interactive lessons. Once you have defined this space, think about where students will sit around the classroom. How many students will you have and how can you optimally fit them in your given space? What's the ideal way to set up their desks—in rows, pairs, small groups? Where will your desk and belongings go?

Giving lots of thought and planning to the design and layout of your classroom will make transitions (such as having students come together for an interactive lesson, go to a laptop cart, or even line up for lunch) effortless and routine. Just remember, you can always rearrange your classroom if it means making it a more efficient and environmentally sound space for you and your students.

CHAPTER 2:

MAKING THE MOST OF YOUR
Interactive Whiteboard

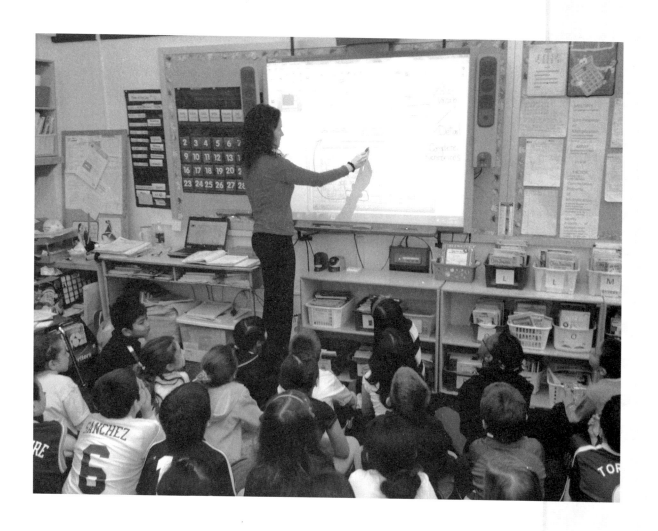

Have you had the experience of walking into your classroom on the first day back from summer vacation to find a strange-looking whiteboard occupying a large space of your classroom wall? "What is this newfangled contraption?" you're thinking. "And what am I supposed to do with it?"

The interactive whiteboard (IWB) is a digital display board that looks similar to a dry-erase board, except you won't be using markers on it. Instead, this electronic whiteboard hooks up to a computer (or laptop or tablet) through a universal serial bus (USB) connection and displays the computer's images through a projector. You and your students can manipulate the images and content on the board using either a digital pen or just a finger—no mouse required! The touch-sensitive display allows users to interact with material on the board in ways that could not have been done before.

So what's so special about interacting with material on an IWB? The proof is in the numbers and in the engagement of students. Recent studies have shown that using IWB technology in the classroom not only increases student engagement, it also puts more focus on content-rich activities that can ultimately result in an increase in test scores (Swan, 2008).

Here's the best part: You can use your interactive whiteboard for nearly any and every lesson that you can imagine. From math to writing to science and social studies, and even art and design, you can utilize your IWB to create eye-catching and engaging lessons. For a list of 10 instant lessons you can do on your whiteboard, see page 34.

In addition to lessons, you can also use your interactive whiteboard to help manage your classroom in innovative ways. If you let it, the interactive whiteboard can be a wonderful teaching partner that will change the way you prepare and teach your lessons—even how your classroom runs from day to day. You just need to invest a little time and work right now to make your experience with the IWB so rewarding, you'll never want to teach without one ever again.

Although your IWB primarily allows you and your students to interact physically with the board, you can also use the IWB in non-interactive ways. Let's say you and your class are studying an entire unit on penguins—their habitat, life cycle, place in the food chain, and so on. While you could no doubt create amazing interactive lessons and activities using pictures, vocabulary words, and anything else you can think of that will bring the unit to life, you could also:

* display PowerPoints and/or Prezi presentations
* watch videos and live broadcast events
* explore maps
* use it for classroom-to-classroom or classroom-to–real world Skyping
* access, explore, and view websites for meaningful and rich discussions
* read digital picture books

Getting to Know Your IWB

When a school purchases interactive whiteboards, the boards are usually installed and set up by a professional company or vendor. However, there may be times when something isn't working the way it's supposed to work and you will have to troubleshoot problems, so getting to know your IWB is very important for day-to-day operations.

I highly recommend asking the technician who installed your IWB to give you a quick overview of the basics, such as turning it on and off. Most technicians will do this automatically, but if they do not, ask. Also, have a digital camera handy so that you can take pictures of the installation as soon as it is completed, for your own records. Snap pictures of the board itself along with the wires coming from the electrical outlets on the wall to where they are connected to your IWB and computer. I also suggest taking pictures of the back of your computer or laptop and even document camera to see where the wires are connected to the board. You may also want to label all the wires so that if one of the connections comes out, you'll know exactly where it belongs. Nine times out of ten, when an IWB will not turn on, the reason is as simple as a connection behind the board or the computer that has come loose or fallen out. A custodian could have accidentally knocked out a connection while cleaning your room or unplugged your computer or IWB in order to plug in a vacuum. When something isn't working or turning on, the very first thing you should do is check all of your connections.

Of course, occasionally you'll find that everything is plugged in correctly, but the board is still not working. In such cases, you may have to ask for help from someone in your school who is more tech-savvy than you. If, however, you've enlisted someone's help and still can't figure out what's wrong with the computer or your interactive whiteboard, you may have to go for further assistance to the vendor from whom you purchased your technology.

Interactive whiteboards usually have warranties that last between one and five years. If there is something physically wrong with the board, it can usually be repaired or replaced free of charge under the company's warranty. Refer to the company's website for contact information or, if you have a technology coordinator at your school, ask that person to help you contact the company to make repairs. The bottom line is, get to know your IWB and its connections so that if something out of the ordinary happens, you can perform a few basic checks before calling for help.

The Multifunctional, Multipurpose "Smart" Board

The interactive whiteboard need not be intimidating, as it can serve many purposes. Even if you're a beginner at using the IWB, if you're familiar with different computer programs, such as PowerPoint, you can actually use the whiteboard successfully right from the get-go.

Think of the interactive whiteboard as a gigantic monitor that's hooked up to your computer. It's really not much different from the computer you use at home or in school, except that everybody can see what you're doing because the screen is so large and its interactive ability allows for a lot more fun and creative use. So if you haven't quite yet mastered how to create interactive lessons for your whiteboard, consider using the board in ways that are more familiar and comfortable. For example, you could show a picture of a spider monkey, a video of a volcano erupting, the front page of the day's newspaper, or a PowerPoint slideshow to supplement a lesson topic. It's an easy way to jump right in and get used to incorporating the technology into your everyday lessons.

Having said this, I do not recommend always using your interactive whiteboard as a glorified projection system. That's a very trivial use for an expensive tool and defeats the primary purpose of the board: interaction.

Classroom Management With the Interactive Whiteboard

Teachers, both seasoned and new, understand that classroom management can make a huge difference in how the day flows from one activity to the next. Classroom management is the key to making a classroom work at a level of efficiency that can—when done with careful thought and planning—make teaching appear to be effortless. Every teacher possesses varying levels of comfort when creating classroom management ideas and actually implementing them. Adding technology into the mix, however, can make the job much easier. Here are some ideas for successfully integrating technology into classroom management.

Classroom Rules

Start using the interactive whiteboard on the very first day of school when you invite students to help you create a set of class rules. (See "Class Rules" on the accompanying CD for a ready-to-use SMART Notebook template.) This classic beginning-of-the-year activity not only encourages students to really think about positive, productive behaviors, but also helps build classroom community.

Gather students in your meeting area in front of the board to discuss what rules are and why they are necessary. Next, elicit rules from students that they feel are important for ensuring a smoothly running classroom environment. Using either a digital pen or the keyboard, list each rule as a student calls it out. List everything and anything—remember, this can be edited later. Of course, you'll want to add any rules that students may not have suggested and that are important to you. Group similar rules by dragging them together and discuss how to incorporate their messages into one rule. In my experience, I've found it beneficial to avoid using negative words, such as *don't* or *no*. It's also a good idea to narrow down the number of class rules to only five, making them more manageable for students to remember.

After you have finalized your class rules, invite students one at a time to the interactive whiteboard to digitally sign the e-document that was created together. Next, email the parents of your class a screenshot of the document along with a little blurb about the classroom rules and expectations. Have parents and students go over them at home for homework to reinforce proper classroom behavior. If you don't have a parent email list early on in the year,

QUICK
TECH TIP

You may also want to generate a list of rules and procedures devoted exclusively to just your classroom technology. For example, you may want to address how to handle and take care of the equipment, what to do if something breaks, or how to properly hold a laptop when walking with it. Remember, it's best to cover all bases and set routines early on in the year. It will only help you and your classroom management in the long run.

simply print out the classroom rules list that was created and send it home for review and discussion. Parents can sign the page to ensure that they've read the document. It's a great way to communicate with parents and, more important, sets very clear expectations for both students and parents.

Classroom Rules

1. Listen when others are talking.

2. Raise your hand if you want to speak.

3. Follow directions.

4. Keep your hands and feet to yourself.

5. Respect others and their property.

QUICK TECH TIP

If your school has an enlarger and laminator, enlarge your new classroom set of rules with student signatures and laminate it for a one-of-a-kind classroom rules poster. Display the poster in a visible area of the room for occasional review during those critical first few weeks of the new school year.

Morning Message and Attendance

One way I have seen teachers use the interactive whiteboard effectively has been when students are just walking into the classroom at the start of the day. We all know how chaotic those first few minutes can be. As a teacher, you can be pulled in twenty different directions at the same time. Limit the chaos by creating a morning-message slide and combine it with your attendance for even more efficiency.

Your morning message could contain directions for what students can do right away, such as deposit important letters or forms in your inbox, pick a new independent reading book from the class library, or hand in homework or assignments. By establishing this as part of your morning routine, students will get into the habit of automatically checking the interactive whiteboard for your instructions. Not only will this teach students responsibility, it will also save you precious time to focus on more important matters.

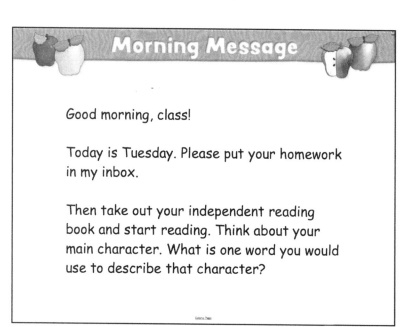

QUICK TECH TIP

You can display both the morning message and classroom attendance pages side by side on the SMART Board using the Dual Page Display feature. In the SMART Notebook menu toolbar, click on **View** > **Dual Page Display** > **On**. Alternatively, you can click on the View Screens icon and select Dual Page Display.

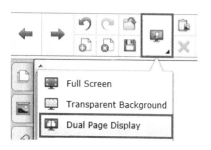

QUICK
TECH TIP

After creating your attendance file with students' names on the interactive whiteboard, save it to your desktop for easy access in the morning. Remember: Do not save the file after students have moved their names, so that when you open the file the next day, the names will be reset under the "Absent/Out/At Home" column.

At the same time, you can also set up your interactive whiteboard to take attendance—without your assistance. On the board, create a T-chart with the headings "Present" and "Absent" (or "In" and "Out" or "In School" and "At Home"). Type each student's name in its own text box and place the names in alphabetical order under the Absent/Out/At Home column. As students arrive and begin to unpack and get settled, have them come up to the interactive whiteboard and drag their names to the Present/In/In School column. When students have all settled down, you can then glance up at the board and officially take attendance—in a fraction of the time that it normally takes. (See "Morning Message_Attendance" on the CD for a ready-to-use SMART Notebook template.)

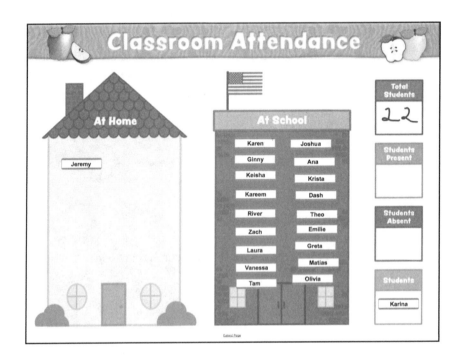

QUICK
TECH TIP

For a variation on interactive attendance, use a digital camera to take a picture of each student and save the picture files on your computer. Instead of listing students' names on the attendance board, use their digital pictures as a fun, visual alternative. This can help students in pre-K or kindergarten who are just starting to learn to recognize their names in print.

Interactive Calendar and Daily Schedule

For many teachers in the primary grades, the daily calendar is a learning-rich part of their morning ritual. In addition to teaching children about months, dates, and days of the week, the daily calendar can also be used to teach a variety of math skills, such as counting, estimation, place value, and problem solving. It can also be used to record daily weather statistics and graph trends in temperatures over the course of time. Of course, the calendar is a natural place to note special days, such as birthdays, field trips, holidays, and more. Incorporating technology into this daily routine opens it up to becoming more interactive and much more dynamic.

Use the SMART Notebook file "Monthly Calendar" (on the CD) to help keep track of the date, the days of the week, months of the year, special events, and more. You can even create your own slide and save it along with the originals. Invite students to the board to drag numbers representing the correct date onto the calendar and keep track of the number of school days by tallying on a chart. There is also a "Weather Calendar" Notebook file on the CD. Take it a step further by linking your favorite weather site to the Notebook file so that you can look at the professional forecast and record the weather right on the calendar.

QUICK
TECH TIP

If you teach younger students (Pre-K to Grade 2), invest in a finger-pointer stick, which can be found at school-supply stores everywhere. The finger-pointer stick acts as an extension to smaller students' hands, helping them reach all corners of the interactive whiteboard and open various tools associated with the board for interactive use. The stick not only helps students focus better, it also helps them practice dexterity and develop motor skills. Plus, the student who gets to hold the pointer and use it on the board becomes a rock star for a moment.

From the interactive monthly calendar, move on to reviewing the daily schedule. (See "Daily Schedule" on the CD for a ready-to-use SMART Notebook template.) Children feel much more at ease when they know what's coming up during the day. This is a great way to conclude the entire morning routine so that everyone is ready to move on to the next activity.

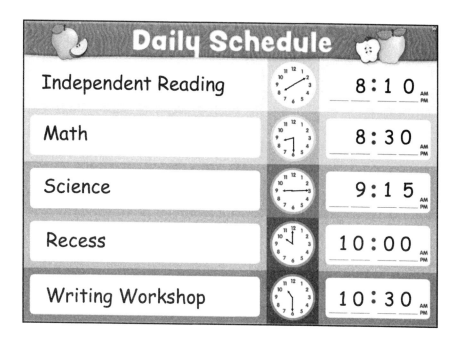

Daily Schedule

Independent Reading		8:10 AM/PM
Math		8:30 AM/PM
Science		9:15 AM/PM
Recess		10:00 AM/PM
Writing Workshop		10:30 AM/PM

QUICK TECH TIP

When using your IWB, make sure it stays on for the duration of the task. However, keep in mind that most projector bulbs are quite expensive (usually around $300 to $500), so know when to turn off your system. You don't want your entire system running during your lunch hour or when the class is out of the room during their gym period. Conserve your bulb to maximize its life.

Classroom Jobs

What better way to empower students (especially younger ones) and teach them about responsibility than to assign them classroom jobs? Students itch to obtain coveted classroom jobs, whether it's the line leader, the closet monitor, or the end-of-day sweeper. Regardless of the job, students like to get involved. And let's face it, running a classroom is much easier when students do their part. And they should—after all, it is their classroom, too!

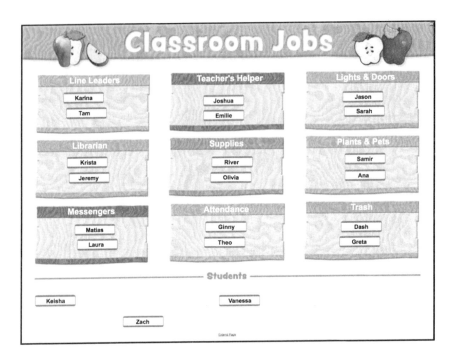

A fun way to organize and assign classroom responsibilities is to use your interactive whiteboard each month. Simply open the "Classroom Jobs" SMART Notebook file on the CD and type in students' names on the name tags provided. You can then drag students' names to their assigned jobs. Alternatively, you can add students' pictures to the corresponding jobs. You can edit or manipulate jobs as you see fit, perhaps even allowing students to get involved in the organization and assigning process. Sometimes I like to elicit ideas from the class as to what jobs may be good for a particular student or have students nominate classmates for certain jobs (especially for those students who may not have had a turn at a particular job). I teach students to say, "I think Denise would make a good line leader because . . ." or, "I nominate Harvey to be our office monitor because . . . ." Not only does this help develop a conversation about responsibilities, it fosters a thinking process based on personalities and abilities.

Finally, save your work and print out the file to display on your bulletin board during that month. Students will get a kick out of seeing their names or pictures next to their job for that month, and it will foster a sense of pride as they perform their daily classroom duties. (If you assign jobs on a weekly basis, follow the same process week by week.)

Seating Charts for Differentiated Group Work or Projects

Seating charts are something most teachers use for their own reference. But now you can use an interactive whiteboard to show students where they need to be.

Use the SMART Notebook "Seating Chart" template (on the CD) to group students as desired. Simply insert your students' names and/or their digital pictures in the file. Displaying the seating chart on the interactive whiteboard quickly shows students where they need to be, thus getting them on task in a shorter time frame. The best part about using your IWB for a seating chart is that it is completely interactive; you can easily arrange partners, table groups, or even differentiated groups at any time and create the best working relationship possible. Simply slide the name of a student (and/or his or her digital photo) to the appropriate place on the chart. For example, place students' names or pictures in the teacher box to let them know they'll be working directly with you for that particular lesson practice. It's a simple yet highly effective way to manage where your students will go to work.

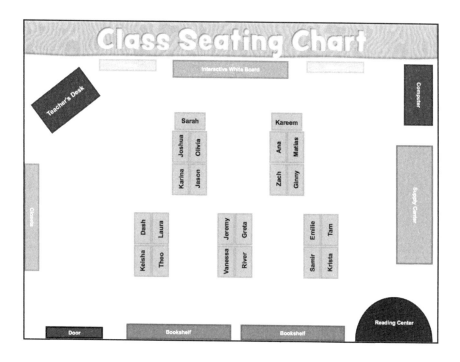

To link a website to a picture on your SMART Notebook slide, right-click on the picture that you have placed on a slide and click "Link..." Next, type or copy and paste the URL (web address) into the Address bar. A small blue globe will appear at the bottom left-hand corner of the image. Click on the blue globe icon to go directly to that website. (Make sure you're connected to the Internet.)

Task Directions

This tip is one of my favorite uses for an interactive whiteboard. It's simple and takes just a few seconds to post on your IWB. Back when I first started teaching, one of the suggestions my principal gave me after a formal observation was to leave the directions for a task up on the (then) dry-erase board after a mini-lesson. Students could then easily refer back to directions, especially if there are multiple tasks for them to accomplish. Since then, I've always written up a "To-Do" list for students' referral. Fast-forward nearly a decade, and technology has replaced my dry-erase markers—and chalk, too. (Think about it: Some students in the primary grades wouldn't even know what a chalkboard is!) These days, I still post directions, but now I use my IWB to list what I expect students to do.

Here's how you can quickly set up your task-directions list: After you create your mini-lesson using your IWB's software, simply add a last slide for that all-important To-Do list. For added fun and interaction, you can also list websites that can be integrated into your lessons, especially if you are using technology in those activities that align to the Common Core. You may even want to list specific software students could use to produce their work, such as Microsoft Office programs or online interactive sites like Prezi or Museum Box. For review, you can also bullet-point the highlights or main points of your lesson.

Class To-Do List

- Get your writing folder.
- Take out the piece you're working on.
- Add more details to your writing.
- For example, if you're describing a day at the playground, you might describe the day (sunny, cloudy, cold, windy). You might also describe the playground. What did you see? What sounds did you hear? Use as many senses as you can to describe what you notice.

If you have students working in groups to complete a task, create a check-box section at the bottom of the To-Do list that has all the groups that are working. Assign one student from each group to come up to the IWB and check off when that group has finished. This will give you a quick visual as to who is done and who is still working.

Setting up a To-Do list on your IWB allows students to refer back to the list as many times as needed (no matter how intricate the tasks may be) and get back to work without struggling to remember what you told them to do (or asking you the directions over and over). Any added resources or suggestions that you list can also motivate students to expand on their work and perhaps even take that next step to create something that exceeds expectations. (See "To-Do List" on the CD for a ready-to-use SMART Notebook template.)

Behavior Management

I suspect most teachers would agree that managing behavior in a classroom setting is one of the most challenging aspects of teaching. Not only does it take a lot of time and energy away from the work that needs to get done, but the types of behavior we see in the classroom can change from month to month and certainly from year to year, calling for different classroom-management styles to be put into action.

One very nice and effective behavior-management technique that I have seen work is the "Change the Color Card" behavior chart. The behavior chart (usually a pocket chart) is often placed in front of the classroom and tracks students' behavior during the course of the day. Most behavior charts use several colors to reflect specific behaviors that occur in class. For example, the traffic light system uses green to mean "great job—keep doing what you're doing," yellow to indicate a warning or "slow down and think about your behavior," and red to stand for "stop right now" or "contact parent/guardian." Although behavior charts are generally found in the lower grades (Pre-K through Grade 2), this tactic can also be used with students in the higher grades to achieve a desired level of respectable behavior.

As a technology cluster teacher, I have occasionally taught in regular classrooms to substitute for a teacher. From my own experience, those teachers who use this type of classroom-management system typically have better-behaved students compared to teachers who do not use any type of visual behavior-management system. When a teacher asks a student to change his or her card from green to yellow or from yellow to red, the act of physically changing the card drives home the message that the student needs to alter his or her behavior for the better.

Regardless of what type of system you have in place and the color that corresponds to each of the consequences, this classroom-management system can be created and then attached digitally to all the lessons you do on your interactive whiteboard. Instead of using a physical chart that hangs in front of the room, just use the SMART Notebook "Behavior Management" template (on the CD) to help track behavior digitally. This virtual behavior chart works the same way as the physical chart and can be attached to the end of any of your interactive lessons.

For instance, say you're presenting a visually engaging interactive lesson on your IWB and one student is having a side conversation with someone else. You can stop the behavior right away by taking a time-out, clicking on the last slide (your behavior-modification slide), and asking the student to drag over an infinitely cloned yellow card (the warning card), and place it over the default green card under his or her name. Chances are that student will immediately stop what he or she is doing, allowing you to get back to your lesson and back to work. What makes this approach even more effective is that all of your interactive lessons will contain a record of students' behavior during those lessons. If you notice a pattern with certain students, you can then call in their parents for a discussion and let them view the lessons that their child wasn't so focused on. It may also be a clue to comprehension concerns; students often lose focus and act out when they do not understand what is being taught.

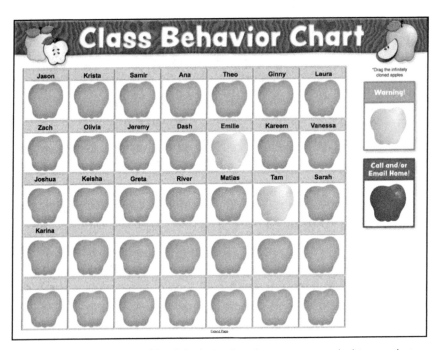

Save a copy of the master file of the behavior chart onto your desktop so that you can continuously copy and paste the digital behavior chart into all of your IWB lessons. This way, you'll always start fresh and won't have to recreate the chart over and over again.

To personalize the interactive behavior chart, take a digital photo of each of your students and place it on the chart along with the color-coded cards and nameplates. You can also take digital notes on specific behaviors right on the slide (for example, "John was talking" or "Lea was calling out"). Once you click Save, you'll have your digital behavior chart saved along with your lesson.

Independent IWB Hands-on Work as a Reward

The interactive whiteboard is such a popular tool for students that you might consider using it for positive reinforcement. (In fact, any of your technology equipment can be a powerful student motivator.) This particular strategy allows students who are less than interested in a topic or who are easily distracted or who may have a behavior modification in place to have a chance at working on the IWB all by themselves. Rewarding these students when they behave appropriately encourages them to become more involved during lessons, making them more likely to succeed.

One of the more effective ways I have found to reinforce positive behavior is to surprise students with something fun to do. Don't announce beforehand that you'll be rewarding students who are paying attention, cooperating, participating, and so on. Instead, keep an eye out for those students

who could use a boost of positive reinforcement and, when they display the kind of behavior you desire, surprise them after the lesson with a trip to the interactive whiteboard to work on material you've just covered. Explain to the students what behavior you saw and why they are being rewarded. You might say, "I noticed that you were trying really hard to pay close attention today" or "I liked how you were sitting so nicely at the meeting area with everyone today." As an added bonus, take a minute or two to work one-on-one with the students so they will feel very important and will likely repeat the good behavior or work ethic in the future. Not only will this build up their confidence, but they'll also feel that you care about them—something that could have a lasting impact over the course of the school year and beyond.

QUICK TECH TIP

Set aside a little time once a week for two or three students who you feel have earned the privilege to use your IWB to play interactive games. (Don't forget that your IWB is attached to the computer, so students can play educational and recreational games on it.) Invite them to join you during lunchtime to eat and then play on the IWB. It's amazing how something that takes just a little of your time can impact students and their drive to succeed. Those same students whom you are rewarding may in turn repay you later on with added confidence, participation, respect, and perhaps even technological assistance.

Virtual Instant-Feedback Exit Cards

Another great way to use your interactive whiteboard on a daily basis is to get instant feedback from students about a lesson through exit cards—virtual ones, of course. With traditional exit cards, students write an answer to a given problem, record something new that they've learned, or ask a question about the lesson that was just taught. While this gives teachers a quick assessment of students' learning, the process itself can also be time-consuming. After all, the teacher has to read each exit card and note who understood a topic and who is still struggling. Combining the exit-card system with your interactive whiteboard, however, allows you to gather some pertinent data about your students in a whole new way. You'll easily be able to see who understood a lesson, who needs a little bit more help, and who didn't get it at all and may need extra support during the next or follow-up lesson.

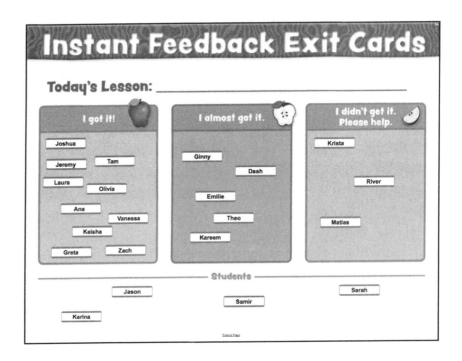

To create virtual exit cards on the interactive whiteboard, set up a table with three columns. Next, label the three columns as follows: "I got it!," "I almost got it!," and "I didn't get it. Please help." (You can also use the ready made "Feedback Exit Cards" file on the accompanying CD, and even edit the file to your liking.) Add your students' names or digital pictures on the side of the board. At the conclusion of a lesson, ask students to come up to the board—one small group at a time or however you see fit—to move their name or picture over to the column that best describes how well they understood the lesson.

NOTE: When implementing exit cards on your IWB, take into consideration how well your class works together. This may take a while to figure out at the start of a new school year. Some teachers may not feel comfortable having their students come up to the board in such a public manner, and some students may feel embarrassed to put their name under a particular category, and that would defeat the purpose. It usually helps to first have an open discussion with the class about how important it is to learn from one another. If you address the idea that everyone in the classroom is there to help one another learn, you'll find that students will be more likely to go to the board and be honest about whether or not they understood something. When I have used a virtual exit-card system, I have noticed that students who were honest about not understanding a concept were approached by classmates who offered peer-to-peer help . . . and when that takes place, you know you did something right.

Effectively Using the Widget Timer

The widget timer in SMART Notebook versions 10 and up could possibly be one of the best interactive tools you can use with your class—whether it's during a lesson, group work, independent work, or a test. You can search for an appropriate timer by clicking on the Gallery icon in SMART's Notebook software. Once you decide on a timer you'd like to use, simply drag it to the workspace area and set it to the time desired.

The timer widget helps students understand the concept of time management. Not only does it keep them focused and on task, it also makes them aware of the passing time and encourages them to plan out the time they actually have to work on a task—something that's very hard for younger students to understand. Say you give your class five minutes to work on a particular task. Train them to refer to the interactive whiteboard to check how much time is left and to keep moving forward to accomplish their work in the amount of time given to them. At the end of the allotted time, a beeper will go off, signaling that time is up. (Remember to turn on your speakers!) Using the interactive timer will enable students to use their time more efficiently and, ultimately, more effectively.

The interactive timer can also benefit adults. Many teachers think that an interactive whiteboard in the classroom is useful only with kids. Not so. You can use your IWB and timer during professional development workshops to help you manage time with other teachers or even during parent-teacher

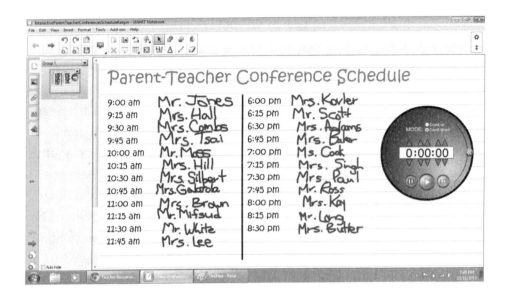

conferences. When meeting with students' parents, you can put the schedule that you have created on your whiteboard. Using the line tools, make a grid, complete with all the time intervals and the parents that you're seeing. Next, go to the SMART Notebook Gallery, pick an interactive timer, and drag it over to the page. Now, you have an instant and interactive way to keep track of the parents you're meeting during parent-teacher conferences and, with the help of your interactive timer, you'll be able to keep your meetings on point and moving along. Most notably, when parents see how many other parents you've already seen (or have yet to see), they'll be more inclined to move the conference along with you.

Digital Classroom Management:
Using Software to Monitor Your Students

SMART Sync, SMART SynchronEyes, or Vision Classroom Management are just a few of the more popular digital classroom-management software programs that are designed for multiple-computer classrooms or computer labs. If your classroom has several laptops or computer stations, using a classroom-management software program allows you to monitor what students are working on and whether or not they are on task. With one glance at your screen, you'll be able to see at once what's on all of your computers.

These types of software programs also allow teachers to put a time-out message on students' screens, so say good-bye to the days when you have to struggle to get students' attention at a moment's notice. Simply send a message such as, "Time out! All eyes on the teacher," and you'll instantly have their attention so you can give additional directions, make a comment regarding someone's work, or start transitioning to a new task. The software has other great time-saving features, including a shutdown button, which shuts down or logs off all of the computers that students are working on. (Just make sure to give students enough warning, so they can save their work before the computers turn off.)

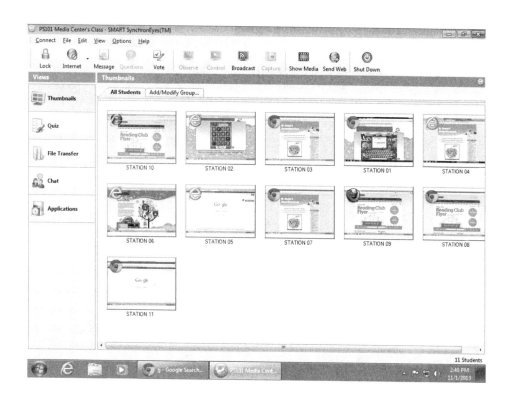

Ten Quick Interactive Lesson Ideas That You Can Do Right Now

Using the interactive whiteboard for classroom management is all well and good, but ultimately, you'd want to use it to make your lessons more fun, more engaging, and more interactive. Here are some lessons you can create in a matter of minutes, motivating your students to become more active participants in the learning process.

1. Letter Formation and Phonics Skills *(Grades K–2)*

Invite young students in kindergarten or first grade to practice letter formation on the interactive whiteboard. Search for "letters" or "lined paper" in the SMART Notebook Gallery to help guide students in writing their letters.

To reinforce phonics skills, place pictures found in the Gallery along with infinitely cloned letters on the interactive whiteboard. Then have students drag each letter next to the picture that has the same beginning sound (for example, *D* for *dog*) or ending sound (*T* for *cat*). Essentially, the pictures and letters become digital manipulatives for students to interact with.

For students in Grades 1–2, type a series of words on the board, making sure each word is in its own text box. Then challenge students to place words in alphabetical order by moving them around on the board or to group them according to a specific phonics element: long vowels, short vowels, word family, and so on.

Liven up word work lessons by using colored pens to help students differentiate and/or highlight consonant blends, vowels, compound words, and so on.

2. Patterns *(Grades K–5)*

Use shapes and numbers to create patterns for students to interpret and continue. SMART Notebook has an Infinite Cloner tool that you can apply to objects so that users can drag unlimited copies of the object. For younger students, start a simple pattern of alternating shapes or colors that they can continue by dragging clones of the objects. This activity can be done with the whole class or in small groups. The level of difficulty can range from colored shapes lined up in a pattern (for kindergarten) all the way up to more complex numbers-oriented patterns (for Grade 5 and up).

3. "Find 7": Daily Editing Practice *(Grades 2–6)*

On your interactive whiteboard, type or write a short paragraph with seven errors, whether in spelling, grammar, or punctuation. I recommend mixing and matching errors intentionally instead of focusing on just one particular type of error. Then challenge students to find the seven errors and make the appropriate corrections—first in their notebooks, then sharing what they notice and making the corrections on the IWB. Use a variety of sources for your paragraphs—from nonfiction articles to fiction and poetry—for review and continuous daily practice. After a few weeks, you'll see students start looking at their own editing with more focus. Continue throughout the year, making the daily edits on the IWB more and more challenging.

4. Book Mind Map *(Grades K–8)*

Whether your class is reading a picture book, a chapter book, or an informational (nonfiction) book, creating a "mind map" on the interactive whiteboard helps facilitate class discussion about the book. Start by searching for an image of the book cover on the Internet, then copying and pasting it to the center of a page or slide on the interactive whiteboard. Prompt students to provide information about the book, such as setting, main characters, problem/solution, particular vocabulary words, and so on. Invite them to come up to the board to add information using lines, arrows, boxes, and circles, or to expand on information that's already on the board. For example, if a student writes the main character's name on the map, call on another student to add details about that character, such as traits or a particular quote from the character. This activity is a great way to get students to think about what they've read, organize their ideas, build connections, link concepts, and so on.

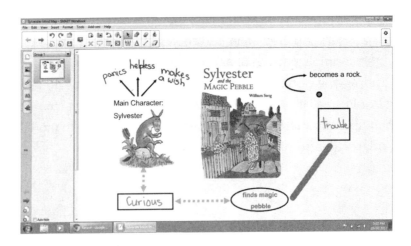

---

5. Pay Three Ways! A Shopping Adventure *(Grades 1–3)*

To prepare for this activity, find an online flyer for your local supermarket and/ or collect several supermarket circulars to distribute to students. Search for pictures of a cash register and various denominations of bills and coins on your interactive whiteboard software or on the web. Place the images on a page or slide on the board and make infinite clones of the money, so students can pull out as many dollars and coins as they want. Next, have students work in pairs to choose an item from the flyer, then figure out three different combinations of money to buy the item. After a few minutes, call on a student pair to share the item they wish to purchase and to demonstrate on the board three different ways to pay for it. Have them slide the money into the cash register.

QUICK TECH TIP

To make the money seem as if it is going into the cash register, click on each image of the money, then click on "Order" and then "Send to Back." Alternatively, you can click on the cash register, click on "Order," and then "Bring Forward."

6. Interactive Timeline *(Grades 3–8)*

When studying history or reading a narrative, creating a timeline on the interactive whiteboard can help students make meaningful connections to historical events or understand how an event unfolds from a complex story. Using the line tool on the IWB software, draw a straight black line (either vertical or horizontal) across the middle of the slide. Then draw as many hatch marks on the line as you need to represent the different times or events on your timeline. To make all the hatch marks exactly the same size, simply clone the first hatch mark you drew and position the copies on the timeline. Finally, engage students in a discussion about what dates, events, and images should be included in the timeline. Don't forget to add a title as well. As an alternative, you can pretype the various dates and events on separate text boxes and put them in random order around the center timeline. Then challenge students to come to the whiteboard and put the events into the correct chronological order. Save the timeline for future reference or print out copies for students to use as a study guide.

QUICK TECH TIP

For additional "working space" on the interactive whiteboard, use the Full Screen option or use the keyboard shortcut of Alt+ENTER. This will temporarily hide your toolbars and the side tabs to allow for more interactive working space for you and your students.

7. Math Problem of the Day *(Grades 2–8)*

In advance of meeting with your class for math, type or write the problem-of-the-day question on your interactive whiteboard with the answer at the bottom of the screen. Next, click on the Screen Shade icon to hide the answer, showing only the question on the screen. When discussing the solution with your class, use different-color pens to highlight, underline, or circle particular key words or phrases in the problem itself. Finally, after students have worked out the solution, click on the Screen Shade to reveal the answer.

8. Vocabulary Hangman *(Grades K–8)*

Use this popular game to review vocabulary and/or spelling with the whole class or a small group. On your interactive whiteboard, set up a page that includes a hangman's noose and all the letters of the alphabet. You may want to distinguish between consonants and vowels by making the vowels a different color. Make each letter an infinite clone so that kids can drag each letter any number of times. You could also draw the various parts of the "man"—head, body, two arms, two legs, and so on—beforehand so kids could just drag them to the noose as well. Play this game to review sight words, word families, content-area vocabulary, or even books the class has read (for example, characters' names, settings, and so on).

9. Multiple Choice Quiz *(Grades 1–8)*

SMART Notebook software includes a Lesson Activity Toolkit, which allows you to tap into several premade activities to use with your class. Activities include a matching game, sentence arrange, timeline reveal, word guess, and even a multiple-choice question set. To create your own multiple-choice question set, click on the Gallery tab in the SMART Notebook software and then click on the Lesson Activity Toolkit folder. Next, click on "Activities" and scroll down to "Multiple Choice." A folder will appear with six "Interactive and Multimedia" items. Just click on your preferred color, drag it onto the workable area of your interactive whiteboard, and follow the onscreen instructions to build your interactive quiz. It's a fun and easy way to review learned concepts and to assess quickly what students do or do not understand. If you plan on using the quiz again next year with a whole new class, be sure to save the file on your computer.

10. Classroom Charts

Use your interactive whiteboard to generate teacher- and student-created classroom posters, handouts, and even study guides or notes. Really, what's better than an informational poster that has been created with and by your class? For example, say you created an interactive lesson for writing workshop, and on the last slide, you listed the steps of the writing process out of order. You then asked students to come up to the board and drag the steps to put them in correct order. After completing the lesson, you can print out the writing process that you and your class just worked on and (a) send home copies for each student, (b) staple a copy into each student's writing notebook, or (c) enlarge the printout into a poster-sized chart to hang up for easy reference. Many times while using your IWB during a lesson, you'll find that the material you and your students have created is just as good—if not better—than the generic posters that can be bought at a teacher store. That's because the material you create tends to be more on point and tailored to your unit, lesson, or lesson objectives.

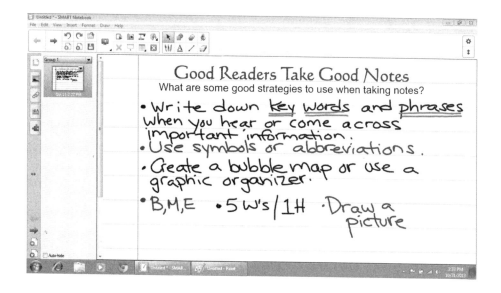

QUICK TECH TIP

SMART Exchange (http://exchange.smarttech.com) is a fantastic standards-aligned resource for ready-to-use lessons and lesson templates in any area of the curriculum—perfect for newbies to the interactive world of teaching. These lessons are created for teachers by teachers and by SMART and some educational publishers. Simply sign up for a free account and you'll be on your way to downloading shared lessons from around the world. If you're eager to start using your interactive whiteboard right away, SMART Exchange is the way to go. Its file-sharing network lets you search by subject, grade level, and file type, so you'll never run out of great interactive ideas!

CHAPTER 3

USING DOCUMENT CAMERAS TO
Enhance Learning

Think back to the "olden" days before technology entered the classroom . . . How did you model how to properly punctuate a piece of writing, demonstrate how to tackle a word problem, or even showcase a student's exemplary work? Odds are, you probably had to rewrite the piece of writing or the math problem on the board or on chart paper so the whole class could see. Later, you might have laid a transparency sheet on an overhead projector and written on it using a special marker, being careful not to accidentally erase what you'd written as your hand moved across the sheet.

In many classrooms today, the document camera—a digital video camera that captures and displays images of flat and 3-D objects on a screen or on the interactive whiteboard—has replaced the overhead projector. Any object placed under the document camera lens is projected and magnified onto the IWB, effectively making that sample piece of writing or math word problem or even a chemistry model visible to everyone, no matter where they are in the classroom.

Five Ways You Can Use Your Document Camera Right Now

Connected to a projector, a document camera is one of the easiest and quickest ways to integrate technology into your teaching. Simply attach the camera to your computer and/or an LCD projector, and you're on your way to actively engaging students in their learning. Here are some quick ideas for how you can use the document camera right now:

1. Showcase Students' Work

One of the most obvious and wonderful ways to utilize a document camera is to display on your interactive whiteboard something that is *not* digital. Say you have just finished teaching a lesson on how to effectively use quotes in a dialogue sequence, and the class is now busy applying that lesson into their writing. As you circulate through the room looking over students' work, you notice one student who is using that particular skill rather well. Ask the student if it would be all right to show the class what he or she has on the paper. (Some students are rather shy about their writing and would rather pass on such a request.) If the student is okay with it, bring the paper to your document camera to project it onto your interactive whiteboard. Once the work is displayed on the board, you can use the highlighter tool to highlight specific sections or use any of the digital pens to circle or underline something you want students to focus on. This way, students can see what their classmates are doing and possibly get ideas from them as well. You can also do this to build the confidence of students who normally struggle by showing their good work on the IWB and to motivate other students into creating exemplary work.

When showcasing a student's work, consider using the screen capture tool on your interactive whiteboard's software to take a snapshot of the work. You can then place a copy in the student's portfolio and use it as evidence of the student's progress. This can also be useful when working with small, differentiated groups at your IWB. You could take a screenshot of the work you did together as a group and print out copies for them to take home or add to their portfolio. It's a quick and easy way to show off some of the great work you and your students have created.

2. Annotate Authentic Text

Use digital ink to mark up authentic texts—whether it's a book, newspaper, or magazine article—that you display via the document camera. This works well when studying how an author uses imagery or descriptive language, for example, or when looking for evidence in a piece of text to answer related questions. To do this, open your interactive whiteboard software (e.g., SMART Notebook or Promethean ActivInspire), place the text under the document camera, and then select the digital camera icon on your IWB's toolbar. This will launch an image of the text directly onto the board. Now, you can use the pen tools to digitally write over the page—without actually marking up the original paper. For example, when demonstrating close reading, you might point out certain ways that an author uses craft in a text by underlining the use of imagery or circling a particular word choice. After you have digitally marked up a piece of text on the board, use the screen capture tool to save your annotations for future reference. You can also print out the screen capture to display on a bulletin board or make copies to send home with students to use as a study guide.

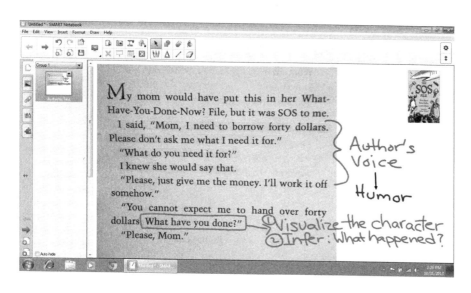

3. Build Vocabulary

A document camera can also come in handy when teaching students how to use context clues to figure out vocabulary in a passage. This works especially well when perusing a social studies or science text. You can pick any type of book (textbook or nonfiction) or newspaper or magazine article and place it under your document camera for instant use. Activate the document camera icon through the IWB software's toolbar to display the text on the board. As you read the passage together as a class, use the highlighter tool to highlight any unfamiliar words you might come across. You might even call on one or two students to come to the board and highlight words they don't know. Next, have a student underline words or phrases in the text that clue the reader in to what the word(s) might mean. Finally, rewrite the vocabulary word on one side of the board along with the definition based on the context clues.

QUICK TECH TIP

If possible, look for multiple levels of text complexity to differentiate your reading lessons. Choose three different leveled passages for students, then invite your target group to the interactive whiteboard and work closely and directly with them for additional support.

4. Weekly Math Practice

You can use your document camera for a weekly fun math-fact practice and quick assessment. On a sheet of paper, write 25 quick math-fact problems, five questions on each line. Place the sheet under the document camera and click on the document camera icon on the SMART Notebook toolbar to display it on the board. Add a timer widget from the Notebook Gallery (search key word *timer*) on the screen, then use the screen shade tool to hide the math-fact practice sheet until you are ready to reveal it to the class. Next, hand out a blank answer sheet (prepared in advance) to each student and set the timer to one minute. Reveal the 25-question set, start the timer, and direct students to solve as many problems as they can until time is up. When the timer goes off, cover up the question set with the screen shade. Within a few minutes, you'll be able to assess who knows their basic math facts and who needs more practice.

You can also put math manipulatives under the camera and invite younger students to use them to show how they worked out a problem. This would hugely benefit your kinesthetic learners.

---

5. Handwriting and Letter Formation Practice

Let's face it—handwriting is quickly becoming a lost art because of the heavy integration of technology. But why not use technology to help bring back good handwriting skills? Use your document camera with pre-K and kindergarten students to demonstrate the proper way to form letters and continue all the way through cursive writing for Grades 3 and up. With the document camera, all students can easily view how to correctly hold the pen and in what order to make the lines or curves to form each letter.

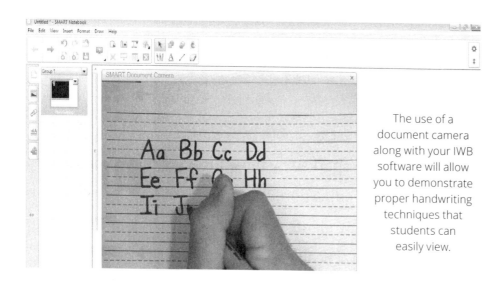

The use of a document camera along with your IWB software will allow you to demonstrate proper handwriting techniques that students can easily view.

QUICK TECH TIP

Take this idea a step further by creating your own interactive letter formation and practice slides on the whiteboard. After demonstrating proper techniques when forming letters, have students come up to the IWB to practice what they've learned on the big screen! Simply type in "handwriting" in the Notebook Gallery search box to find premade handwriting worksheets and lined paper—the virtual kind, of course! Students of all abilities can come up to your IWB to practice their handwriting.

CHAPTER 4:

The Flipped Classroom

What You Need to Know

"Flipping" a classroom is a relatively new idea that was directly sparked by the infusion of technology into the field of education. The premise of the flipped model is relatively simple: Students watch a teacher-created video lesson at home, then do practical work or problem solving—what is traditionally homework—when they return to school the following day. Students work in the classroom individually, in pairs, or in small groups to complete activities that reinforce the concept they learned the previous evening. This way, teachers can circulate the classroom to help students and explain potentially difficult concepts to minimize frustration. A 2012 survey of 409 teachers in grades K–12 by We Are Teachers found that 30 percent of teachers have flipped their classroom at least once.

As with any new teaching model, the flipped classroom has its pros and cons. If done correctly, however, flipping can potentially make class time more focused and meaningful. Let's take a look at some of the advantages and some of the challenges of flip teaching.

The Pros:

✿ Students can learn at their own pace by watching, pausing, and re-watching lessons at home and/or with outside support from a tutor or parent, if necessary. The additional time given to absorb the material could, in fact, be the key to better comprehension.

✿ Teachers can circulate through larger classes without compromising time spent on delivering a lesson. They have more time to work with students on a differentiated, one-on-one basis. Students can ask better questions and have more meaningful discussions with a teacher if they don't understand the material they watched during the previous evening. This allows for deeper understanding of material.

⚙ Parents can gain a better understanding of what is being taught and find appropriate ways to assist their child for additional support if needed. There is absolutely no question as to what students are learning and what they are expected to know.

⚙ Although initially it may take teachers additional time to record a lesson, once a lesson is recorded and saved, it can be used again down the road. Teachers can build and store a library of lessons for important study practices and test review. Students can relive a teacher's lesson word for word by watching the video over and over again on demand.

⚙ Administrators and content coaches can view lessons and offer suggestions or guidance on various lesson topics. This can be an additional piece of professional development that can help teachers grow at a much faster rate.

⚙ All posted teaching lessons are always available, even for students who are absent from school.

The Cons:

⚙ Is there enough technology to go around? Does every student have a computer or tablet at home from which to view the assigned lesson? Flip teaching could inadvertently widen the digital divide in classrooms if not handled carefully. Of the teachers surveyed by We Are Teachers, 47 percent noted that students do not have access to the technology to view online lessons. One option might be to have students view the lessons at the school library or computer lab.

⚙ What steps will be taken for the student who does not or cannot watch the video lesson at home? How will that affect the class work the following day for that individual? What if several students don't watch the lesson? How should teachers address this potentially disruptive issue?

⚙ Although teachers would be differentiating during in-school work and support, the impact of differentiation at home while students watch lessons may not be as apparent. This could potentially do more harm than good and could create confusion.

⚙ Is it good teaching practice to have students learn from a computer and not in person from a teacher? Teachers can often tell just by looking at students' faces whether or not a lesson is clear and can adapt their teaching styles accordingly. Without this instant feedback, teachers may not know for quite a while whether their video lessons are successful.

- Not every teacher feels comfortable with technology. So while the idea of a video lesson may sound appealing, the quality of the video will depend heavily on the teacher's creativity and technical know-how.

- There are no long-term studies on the flipped classroom model, so whether or not it is an effective teaching tool is still to be determined.

Before you jump on the bandwagon, here are a few more things you might want to consider:

- Do you have the proper equipment—such as a computer or laptop, webcam, and fast Internet connection—to create and upload your lesson videos? The survey by We Are Teachers revealed that 36 percent of teachers said that they themselves do not have access to the technology needed to develop and deliver lessons online.

- Where will you upload your videos? How will your students access the videos?

- What is your "Plan B," in case of a technological breakdown (for example, Internet outage or a server issue)?

- Will you have the support of administrators in your school to become a lab-site to try out the flipped model?

- How will your parent base react to such a shift in how lessons are taught and how material is worked on?

- How much of your syllabus will you flip?

QUICK TECH TIP

Keep parents in the loop when it comes to your interactive whiteboard lesson by having them download a free version of the SMART Notebook application (http://express.smarttech.com).

SMART Notebook Express allows anyone to view, but not edit, a Notebook file. You can use SMART Notebook to create a lesson that includes a screencast from Screenr[sm] or the Page Recorder feature. Students and their parents can then watch the lesson at home through SMART Notebook Express. This can enhance parent-teacher communication because parents will be aware of lessons and work that you've assigned. It's a win-win situation!

Do your research and start small, perhaps with just one subject area. Logically speaking, math seems to be a good place to start because topics can easily be divided into small chunks—for example, the commutative property of multiplication, or adding fractions with like denominators. This not only makes the lessons manageable to create, but also easily absorbed by students. With this self-paced learning technique, students can pause or play back material for review and slow down the progression of the material to their own learning speed (also known as self-paced differentiation). At school, teachers can then spend the additional time to work with and support those students who need extra guidance even after the previous night's online lesson. Students who are struggling to understand a topic or concept can now have much-needed additional attention to help them grasp the work and tackle it appropriately.

As with anything else in technology, how one uses the tools makes all the difference. If you feel confident with your technology skills and feel that a flipped-classroom approach could make a significant impact on your classroom instruction, why not try it? I believe that the future of education will ultimately include some version of the flipped approach. So, go ahead and be a trailblazer in your school and take the technological leap forward. You may just stumble upon a variation of the flipped model that can make a substantial difference in your students' achievements!

Producing Your Flipped Lessons

Ready to get started? Recording a lesson can be as easy as setting up a video camera in front of your board and teaching a lesson the way you normally would in front of a class—except there would be no students for you to interact with. If you are more comfortable with technology and want to step it up a notch, you can also try Ezvid (http://www.ezvid.com/), a free downloadable program that allows users to create videos, screen recordings, and slideshows. The program allows you to record virtually anything on your computer, edit the video, and then upload to a YouTube account.

Another free web-based service is Screenr (http://www.screenr.com/), which also allows you to capture and record anything you do or say on your computer (for example, demos, tutorials, and presentations). All you need is a microphone or a webcam with a built-in microphone. After you record, you can share the lesson via email or on your website. You can also download the screencast to an mp4 file format and publish your videos to YouTube. Screenr also stores your past screencasts in a video library under your account. If you're ever absent, you can send a link to your Screenr video library to your substitute teacher so that he or she can play one of your lessons right on the interactive whiteboard.

If you have a SMART Board, you can also use SMART Notebook's Page Recording feature, available on versions 10 and up. Click on the Properties tab [⬛], then click on Page Recording to capture what you're doing on the interactive whiteboard. (Note: This feature does not record sound.) You can also use this feature to replay a lesson as you send students off to work independently or in small groups. They can glance up at the interactive whiteboard at any time to review the lesson you just taught.

Once you've recorded your flip lessons, you'll need a website to house your videos. There are many free websites that could serve the flipped-classroom purpose, but probably the best places to upload your videos to are YouTube EDU (http://www.youtube.com/education) and Teacher Tube (http://teachertube.com/). If you are willing to pay a monthly fee for a more professional-looking website without advertisements, check out Yahoo! Web Hosting (http://smallbusiness.yahoo.com/webhosting/).

Engaging Flip-Lesson Ideas You Can Do Right Now

Now that you're all set to record your lessons, here are some ideas for flipped instruction that you can start with:

1. Math, Math, Math

Create an interactive lesson on your interactive whiteboard for presentation purposes only (remember, no students are in front of you while you're recording your lesson). For example, you might do a lesson on multiplication by showing arrays or on fractions by using parts of shapes. For younger students, you could show how to add on a number line or how to tell time using an interactive whiteboard clock. You can manipulate objects on the whiteboard as you model and deliver your lesson.

2. Note-taking

With the Common Core pushing for an understanding of high text-complexity levels, especially in nonfiction pieces, students need to know how to take good notes and pull information from a variety of intricate texts. Taking notes effectively is a skill that requires many sessions or class periods to teach. Using flip teaching is a great way to break down the skills into smaller, more manageable lessons that will ultimately allow students to gain a deeper understanding of increasingly complex text material. This all happens naturally because you will be able to work with increasingly complex texts in class due to the time saved from teaching note-taking as flip lessons.

Below is a list of various strategies for note-taking:

- writing key words and phrases
- abbreviating frequently used words
- using meaningful symbols, such as an arrow to indicate cause and effect or an equal sign to represent equivalent ideas
- using the 5 Ws and H (*who, what, where, when, why,* and *how*)
- drawing pictures and diagrams
- using bullet points

3. The Scientific Method

Use flip teaching to help prepare students for an upcoming science lab experiment. How many times have you had only one class period to talk about an experiment, discuss the scientific method, give out directions, and distribute supplies, only to realize that your 45-minute class period has only 25 minutes left because of all the prep work that needed to be done? Save class time by assigning students a video lesson on the scientific method as well as on lab procedures and etiquette. When they enter the classroom the following day, they can quickly get their supplies ready and conduct the actual experiment, gather data, analyze and synthesize their findings, and so on. This also gives you time to monitor student work and interact more meaningfully with them to foster growth and achievement. Take advantage of technology and flip teaching for any type of prep work that can sometimes eat up more of the class period than you're willing to give up.

QUICK TECH TIP

Combine the introduction to key vocabulary terms along with note-taking strategies. Have students watch your video lesson at home and take notes on the vocabulary that you are introducing. The following day, start the class by having students take out their notes from the previous night to refer to during your lesson and discussion.

4. Building Background Knowledge

Social studies, history, and science have been folded into the Common Core standards for English Language Arts, making it necessary for teachers to find creative ways to infuse academic and domain-specific vocabulary into their lessons. Providing students with a mini-lesson video that introduces key terms and builds background knowledge prior to a history lesson, for example, can help build a solid foundation for students, allowing them to dig deeper into material and gain a better understanding of complex texts.

5. Word-Processing Tutorial

This lesson can be a relatively easy flip, whether you're a technology teacher or a classroom teacher who just wants to teach students how to use a word-processing program so you can focus on the writing process in the classroom. Simply record your lesson using a web-based screen-capture program (like Ezvid or Screenr) and create mini demonstration videos that show how to use the toolbars, format text, add clip art or pictures, save and retrieve files, and even how to use the spell-check feature. When students come for writing workshop the following day, they will have some basic knowledge of word processing and can dive right into writing and publishing their pieces on laptops, desktops, or tablets.

Once you understand the reasoning behind the flipped classroom, you can then decide how and on what level you'd like to use it. A flip approach does not have to be done every day in every subject. Realistically speaking, that may be hard to do and even unnecessary (especially in the beginning, as you and your students are just getting used to it). However, if you feel that the flipped approach can easily be implemented with your students and you have the technology to support it, go for it. Just remember to start off small; you don't want to overwhelm yourself so that you give up too soon. Start by trying it out once a week so you can gauge how it is accepted by all of the players involved. This will also allow you to work out the kinks, if any. Practice and experimentation make perfect.

QUICK TECH TIP

Record two-minute tutorials that explain and demonstrate Common Core–specific lessons. Focus on one specific skill that you want students (and parents) to work on together. Parents will appreciate getting some insight into what their kids are learning at school.

CHAPTER 5:

Mobile Learning

With Mobile Devices and Tablets

It's no secret that what was once an iconic idea—desktops and laptops in the classroom—is quickly becoming outdated. More school districts are starting to move away from them and focusing their attention on iPads and other similar mobile tablets. So why is this new fad taking off at such an incredible speed?

Tablet computers, including the iPad, are smaller than traditional laptops, are very portable, and offer quite a punch when it comes to speed, power, reliability, and user-friendly interfaces. These mobile devices allow students to perform tasks in ways that were not an option in the past. For instance, students can now take notes on their tablets in class, email the notes to themselves, store them in the "cloud," or send them to other students in their working group or who may be absent. Students can research material online, expand and collaborate on their ideas using a word-processing app (such as Google Drive), and share it out to anyone in a heartbeat. (Back when I was a student, I used something called carbon paper, and that doesn't come anywhere close to what students can do today!)

These are just some of the reasons why these mobile devices are becoming so popular and in high demand. Although the tablet revolution is affecting the education world in ways previously unimaginable, there are a number or pros and cons to having, using, and incorporating tablets into a classroom.

The Pros

⚙ Tablets are lightweight and very portable so they can easily be moved from class to class. For older students (in middle school and high school), tablets may literally lighten their load as more publishers are putting textbooks in digital format so they can be accessed via tablets.

⚙ Tablets are more affordable than computers or laptops, and some companies offer bulk rates to schools, making them even cheaper. Of course, a school could always opt to start small with a single lab-site class to test how these devices can be incorporated into the curriculum and how teachers and students can utilize them. More devices can then be purchased if the lab site proves successful.

⚙ From pre-K on up, children just seem to know how to use tablets right from the get-go. Take my daughter, for example, who, at the age of 3 was quite the pro at turning on my iPad, sliding over apps with incredible ease, tapping on a game, a drawing app, or video, and keeping herself occupied for some period of time. The remarkable thing was that I never sat down with her and taught her how to use the device. She learned just by watching me and then exploring on her own. Did she accidentally delete an app here and there? Yes, but it wasn't the end of the world. She was learning how to use the device and doing it as if it were second nature. Although some adults may need more time to get acclimated to using the device, teachers will eventually feel quite comfortable using them for various tasks.

✿ There are thousands of free educational apps (short for *applications*) on Apple's App Store or on Android's Google Play. Many of these apps are free because they come with ads or are a bare-bones version of a full app. For a minimal charge (usually $0.99 to $4.99), you can upgrade to an ad-free version or the full working version of the free app. These apps cover a wide range of curriculum areas, including math, science, reading, writing, history, art, music, and so on, and can be used to supplement and/or reinforce your lessons. (See page 58 for a list of recommended apps.)

✿ Many teachers across the country have seen how tablets can engage and motivate students, particularly those with special needs and learning disabilities. These devices offer a different way of learning that combines visual, auditory, and kinesthetic modes with an element of fun.

✿ Perhaps one of the best things about tablets is that they can store hundreds of books in one portable device. Whether through Kindle, iBooks, Storia, or another e-book reader app, teachers can build a whole classroom library in a device and give students access to many e-books, including interactive ones that enhance the reading experience by including videos, animations, and even mini games and quizzes.

The Cons (and Other Challenges)

✿ One huge concern educators have with tablets is the limited battery power. When used in the classroom, constant interactive use and continuous connection to the network can drain the battery even faster. But with the new lithium-polymer batteries powering tablets, students can use them throughout the day on a single charge. Device settings can also be tweaked for maximum battery life, so that a device can last 10 or more hours on a single charge. And with a tablet cart, teachers can charge a classroom set of tablets in one go.

✿ Given their small size and light weight, tablets can be quite delicate. And kids can sometimes be less than careful about the way they handle these fragile instruments. The best solution is to purchase additional accessories, such as screen protectors and hard cases, to ensure protection from damage.

✿ What procedures need to be put in place to make sure that the devices are properly stored, charged, and locked up at the end of every day? Security carts are available to house the devices, but can also be quite expensive. Nevertheless, if you are investing in the devices, you'll want to invest in their security as well.

✿ Speaking of security, teachers also need to think about their students' online safety while using the devices. Many schools already have some type of acceptable use policy (AUP) for technology that defines, among other things, appropriate and inappropriate Internet conduct. At the beginning of the school year, be sure to discuss with students the school's and your policies for using technology in the classroom. While most school districts have some type of filter that prevents students from accessing unsuitable websites, it's not always foolproof. Many tablets, however, do come with parental controls that can and should be activated.

✿ Does your school have the necessary technology funds available to purchase a class set of tablet computers? If not, what steps can be taken to secure funding? How much is your school willing to pay for insurance on the iPads and tablets that are purchased? How do you pay for (and get reimbursed for) full-version apps that you would like to install on each tablet? These are just some questions to consider when purchasing tablets for the classroom.

QUICK TECH TIP

Research websites and blogs to find the best educational apps to download and use with your students. Don't overlook apps that are free! To find the latest popular apps, go to search engines such as Yahoo! or Google and type "best free educational apps" or "top 25 free educational apps" in the search box. You'll find lots of lists from teachers and educational publishers that will help you make good, informed decisions on what apps will support you and your students to get the job done.

There's an App for That

iPads and other tablets are only as powerful as the apps that are on them. There is a wide variety of apps for various purposes—calculator apps, e-book reader apps, book-creating apps, social media apps, dictation apps, photo-editing apps, weather apps, even apps that tell you all about other apps! When using tablets, think about the types of apps that will foster in your students a love for learning and creativity. Here are a few apps that are not only popular, but really fantastic learning tools:

Top Educational Apps for Grades Pre-K–2:

* **Sight Words: Kids Learn** – A fun and interactive way to teach students sight words.

* **Articulation Station** – Up to six students can practice proper articulation together in six fun activities.

* **SpellingCity** – A great way to practice spelling in a test or game format.

* **Fast Facts Math** – Helps students sharpen their math facts and provides a detailed progress report, which can be emailed or printed out after each practice.

* **Storia** – Scholastic's very own innovative e-reader app specializes in interactive picture books and series books. Students can manage their own personalized bookshelves and look up words they don't know right on the app itself!

Top Educational Apps for Grades 3–5:

* **King of Math** – Engages students in practicing basic and higher-level math thinking skills.

* **Math Puppy—Bingo Challenge** – A fun way to build up math skills from pre-K through grade school in a bingo-style format.

* **MindMapper** – Allows students to think visually and create brainstorming ideas in a colorful and interactive format in all areas of the curriculum.

* **Brain Quest** – A curriculum-based educational question system that helps kids practice important skills in all areas with challenging questions and brilliant graphics.

* **VocabularySpellingCity** – Students can practice their weekly word-study words through a variety of learning games.

Top Educational Apps for Grades 6–8:

⚙ **Answer Underground** – Allows students to create mobile study groups in all academic areas and get verified instructional help from educators across the globe.

⚙ **Khan Academy** – Offers podcasts and video clips in every academic area at a student's own pace.

⚙ **StudyBlue** – Students can study virtual flashcards, study guides, and material for tests or quizzes anywhere and anytime.

⚙ **SAT: The Official SAT Question of the Day** – Gives students an edge in preparing for the SAT exams.

⚙ **Note Taker HD** – Helps students organize their writing, draw diagrams, and of course, take notes.

Top Educational Apps for Teachers:

⚙ **TeacherKit** – A personal classroom organizer, teacher assistant, and grade book all rolled up in one. Keep tabs on attendance, grades, and even student behavior.

⚙ **iGrade (Teacher's Gradebook)** – This iPad grade book has lots of great bells and whistles that give you a complete data analysis of students in your class. It even allows for an augmented-reality look at your classroom and where students sit.

⚙ **Easy Behavior Tracker for Teachers** – Tracks students' behavior and allows teachers to notify parents directly from the app itself.

⚙ **Common Core by MasteryConnect** – This timely app puts the Common Core State Standards in the palm of your hand by subject and grade level.

⚙ **ShowMe** – Turns your iPad into a portable interactive whiteboard. You can write on it and record your voice to create tutorials for students who have been absent or need extra support.

Cell Phones as Computers

Lately, more and more schools are rethinking their "no cell phone" policies, which they've had in place for a very long time. While this is mostly for safety reasons, some schools are even permitting students to use their smartphones in the classroom. The use of smartphones in education is becoming increasingly popular for two main reasons: First, it instantly puts the Internet and a means of communication directly in the hands of students. Secondly, it doubles, triples, or even quadruples the number of Internet-ready devices that are available in a classroom, especially when students need them for work or research purposes. And, when a school or district doesn't have the funds for more computers, allowing kids to bring their own mobile devices is one way to get technology in the classroom. Likewise, some schools welcome the use of the mobile devices because these devices on the 3G and 4G networks are much faster than the Internet connection speeds that are currently available at school.

While working with sixth graders at our computer lab one day, our Internet suddenly went down. Because we were relying heavily on the Internet for research on that particular day, my students and I were very frustrated when the Internet stopped functioning. When I announced that we'd have to wait until the following week to continue working, one student asked if she could get her smartphone because she could access the Internet on her 3G network. My first impulse was to say no, but then I thought, "Why not?" I allowed her and a few others to go and get their smartphones so that they wouldn't lose any time working on their project. As a result, those who were using their smartphones to do research became surprisingly even more focused and determined to gather their information. It was a huge, albeit accidental, success! As the future continues to unfold, we'll see these types of situations become more and more commonplace in the classroom. In fact, according to a November 2012 article by PewInternet.org, 43 percent of ninth and tenth graders are already using mobile devices, such as smartphones, to look up information online.

What the Future Might Hold

Once upon a time, devices such as smartphones, tablet computers, interactive whiteboards, and document cameras were nothing more than sci-fi imaginings. Nobody could have predicted that students would be reading novels and textbooks on their phones and on tablets. Nobody could have even predicted that education would be so immersed in technology . . . but it is. It would not surprise me if within a few years of the publication of this book, tablet-like devices were on every student supply list for the back-to-school sales. It also wouldn't surprise me to see book bags shrink down in size to house just a tablet and a stylus, instead of several textbooks, notebooks, and pens or pencils. Technology is advancing so fast that our wildest ideas for technology and education could indeed be a reality in the not-too-distant future.

CHAPTER 6:

Communicating and Collaborating
in the Digital World

Perhaps one of the largest impacts technology has in today's world is that it has made communication and collaboration so much easier and more widespread than ever before. With so many resources to pull from, teachers and parents can communicate with each other from anywhere and at any time. Tech tools such as email, class websites, and social media have made it possible for parents to keep close tabs on their children's school life, including homework, tests, field trips, teacher meetings, special events, and so on. And, of course, these same tools work for students as well. How can we harness the power of technology and use these tools effectively to communicate and collaborate better?

One of my favorite online tools is Google Drive (formerly Google Docs), which offers a digital way to house files and folders in the "cloud" for file storage, revisions, and virtual collaboration. Google Drive can be accessed from any device with an Internet connection, so you can lose those flash drives and removable disks! All you need to do is sign in to your Google account (or create a free account, if you don't have one yet), then search for Google Drive.

For collaborative purposes, Google Drive works like this: One person creates a document file and can then invite another person (or as many people as desired) into the document for online, real-time collaboration and editing. This essentially allows two or more people to work on and edit a single shared file simultaneously, and to see the changes and edits that are being made as they happen. In addition, a chat feature right on the document page allows the collaborative group to communicate as the work is being done. So, gone are the days when scheduling a get-together outside of school was an issue. Now, students and/or teachers can meet virtually and get the work done faster and, in many cases, better.

Sharing files on Google Drive is as easy as sending out a secure email invitation. You can opt to share a file so that the other participant(s) can only view it and perhaps make comments, or can view it and actually make changes to the file. Google Drive even allows you to see the revision history from the group and download the file in a number of widely used and popular file formats, such as Microsoft Word, Excel, PowerPoint, and PDF.

So what are some ways you can use Google Drive in the classroom? Here are some ideas:

1. Homework Organizer

Set up a virtual "homework board" via Google Drive and email all the parents in your class an invitation to view the document. With access to this board, parents will never again question whether you assign homework daily—especially when their child comes home and says that there isn't any homework to be done that night. Here's how you can easily set this up:

After opening Google Drive, click on "Create" on the left-hand side of the screen and choose "Document" to create your own weekly homework sheet, or "From Template" to search for homework calendar templates that other users may have already created and shared. (If you don't see the "From Template" option, click on "Connect more apps" and find it there.) Type your homework assignments and due dates onto the document or template. To share the file with parents in your class, click on the "Share" button in the upper right-hand corner of the Google Drive page, enter their email addresses, then click "Done." As you edit the homework form on Google Drive, your students and parents will automatically see the changes. Update the homework board daily or weekly to communicate assignments with ease.

QUICK TECH TIP

To ensure that even those parents (or other users) who don't have Google accounts can access your files, change the Sharing settings to "Anyone with the link." It's not as restrictive as "Private," but only those people to whom you've shared the link can access the files.

2. Class List

Another excellent way to use Google Drive is to create a class contact list of all the students in your class, along with their addresses, phone numbers, parent emails, birthdays, and so on. Parents can update their own information, and students can use it to look up a classmate's contact information. Best of all, only those whom you invite can view or edit the list, essentially keeping the information secure and available only within your class. And really, what's better than having everyone in the class add their own information instead of leaving it entirely up to you or a class parent?

For more details on how to use Google Drive, visit YouTube or Google and search for a "how-to" tutorial. You'll find a variety of helpful tutorials that may spark even more ideas for using Google Drive and Google Calendar. For a fun visual explanation of how Google Drive works, watch http://www.youtube.com/watch?v=eRqUE6IHTEA.

3. Class Calendar

Create a weekly, monthly, or even yearly class calendar with Google Calendar. List vacation days, field trips, birthdays, test dates, parent meetings and workshops, and any other special events related to your classroom. With Google Calendar, you can even allow class parents and other teachers and/ or administrators to add to or edit the calendar you have created. This type of "living document" can also be added to a school website. It's a quick and very effective way to enhance communication between home and school. Start out small, then expand as you find ways to incorporate this technology into your class and beyond the walls of your school!

4. Quick Quizzes and Instant Grading

One of the things teachers don't particularly enjoy is the process of grading quizzes. Although the data gathered can be extremely beneficial, grading quizzes can be tedious and time consuming. So why not use Google Forms and let your computer take over the grading and data analysis process for you?

Google Forms is perfect for creating all kinds of online quizzes—multiple choice, short answers, longer responses, and so on. Simply send students a link to the quiz via email or through the school or class website, and you're on your way to assessing how well they have understood your lesson. Of course, this is ideal if you have access to a computer lab or have a class set of laptops or tablets. But if your class doesn't have enough computers to go around, allow students to take the quiz as part of a take-home assessment.

What makes this process even more exciting? As students complete their test or quiz and click the submit button, you get the results immediately. Data is instantly compiled with the students' scores. You'll be able to see what questions were answered correctly—or incorrectly—along with pie charts and other forms of data analysis, including what percentage of students got each individual question correct or what percentage of students picked any one particular answer/distractor (if you created a multiple-choice quiz). It's like having your own teaching assistant there to do all of the grading for you!

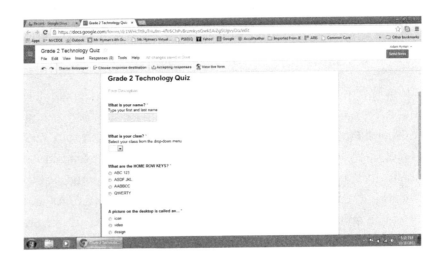

5. More Classroom Management Ideas

There are many more ways you can use Google Drive in the classroom. Use it to create digital reading logs, virtual exit cards, parent surveys, or a classroom library checkout system. You can even use it to gather topic ideas when planning for future professional development.

Virtual Field Trips and Online Chats With Experts

Who doesn't love to go on a field trip? Teachers love field trips because they can get out of the classroom and show their students a whole new world. Students love field trips because it connects material that is being studied in the classroom to the real world. Yet leaving the classroom can sometimes be challenging or even impossible to do. For example, you can't just hop on a bus to go to Egypt to visit the Great Pyramid. Likewise, a good museum that houses ancient Egyptian artifacts or even an expert in Egyptology may not be nearby. In addition to logistical issues, financial reasons can also prevent field trips from taking place. That's where technology can come into play.

With the help of an interactive whiteboard, a good Internet connection, and a webcam with microphone, you can take your class on a virtual field trip and go anywhere and talk to anyone in the world—right in the comfort of your own classroom! A free video chat and instant messaging account, such as Skype (www.skype.com) or ooVoo (www.oovoo.com), will allow your class to communicate in real time via the Internet using a webcam, text, and voice. When you can't physically go somewhere with your students, just set up a Skype or ooVoo conference with an expert in a particular field, and those virtual field trip possibilities are almost endless. You can go on a virtual field trip to a firehouse, an animal hospital, or even a museum without ever stepping outside of your classroom. Want to invite someone in for Career Day but the person's schedule just doesn't allow him or her to be there physically? Simply Skype the person right at his or her workplace!

QUICK TECH TIP

Create a free account to Skype in the Classroom (https://education.skype.com/) not only to connect your classroom to the world, but to incorporate great lessons ideas and projects as well. It's very exciting when you can bring the world into your classroom and learn from a multitude of people and resources!

Think of using your interactive whiteboard or laptop as a way to have your own talk show, with your students as your television studio audience. We've seen people being interviewed on TV using Skype, and now you can do the same thing with your own equipment. Many book publishers, including Scholastic, can set up an author study and Skype session with your class for a fee. Wrap up an author study by Skyping the author of the books that you just focused on for a unit. The author can give your class more insight into why he or she wrote the books, after which your class can have a fantastic question-and-answer session with the author. By the same token, students can go on a virtual tour and interact with an on-the-spot expert. You can even set up a long-distance Skyping pen-pal relationship with a classroom—just about anywhere on the planet. What's the best thing about all these online activities? They integrate many areas of the curriculum and the Common Core, such as reading, writing, researching, and speaking and listening skills.

Collaborating on Common Core Projects

The Common Core State Standards call for students to use technology to conduct research, produce and publish writing, and interact and collaborate with others. Google Drive offers the perfect venue for students in Grades 5 and up to work on online projects. Of course, a Google account must be set up first, but with the proper structure and design, these projects could foster critical thinking, self-differentiation, and online collaboration. You might even want to invite parents to monitor or work with their child on a project. Here are some ideas to get you and your students started:

1. Science or Social Studies Report

Assign students to work in groups of three to create a report on a particular science or social studies topic. This is particularly useful for students to review material or delve deeper into a recently studied topic. Don't give too much direction; let them decide what topic they would like to research and how they want to design their report. Simply provide a scoring rubric and have students create a Google Drive document that includes a planning page, pictures, and any other guidelines that you feel are necessary.

2. Test Review Sheet

Have students get into online collaborative study groups to help prepare for a state test. Students can create their own study guide material that mirrors what is being taught in class, including note-taking strategies and a custom glossary of terms. This is a fun, interactive way for students to review material that was taught throughout the year in any subject.

3. Math How-to

Challenge students to work in pairs to create a slideshow presentation (using PowerPoint or Keynote) that explains how to solve a multistep math problem. Encourage students to explore multiple ways of finding a solution using different problem-solving strategies, such as working backwards, drawing a picture, making a chart, guess-and-check, and so on. Demonstrate how one person in the pair can start a PowerPoint presentation and upload it to Google Drive so his or her partner can access the file as well. They can then collaborate and edit the presentation online. Alternatively, students can also use Prezi, a free cloud-based presentation software (www.prezi.com) that requires a current email address to set up an account.

4. Business Plans

One favorite project I've done with my class is to have students create their own business. Divide the class into groups of about five students each and have them use technology to create their own business cards, design their grand-opening flyers, put together menus for a restaurant, or produce a 30-second commercial to be shown on your interactive whiteboard. Students can use Microsoft Publisher, PowerPoint, Prezi, and various other software. You'll be amazed at what students come up with when they collaborate and are given free rein to use technology.

5. In the News

Have students work in groups of five to seven to create online newspapers. Students can become the writers, editors, and photographers of their own monthly newspaper to be digitally shared out to the entire school. Have them include current events, sports headlines, movie reviews, and more, for a one-of-a-kind online edition.

CHAPTER 7:

Exploring Social Media

Social media web services, such as Facebook and Twitter, can be a quick and easy way to keep communication lines open for an entire school community or even just a single class. Start a school or class Twitter account to see how much it can help spread the word or get things done faster. Using Twitter, teachers and administrators can send out short messages (up to 140 characters in length), such as reminders for when homework assignments and projects are due, news about school or class events, or special service announcements, such as when school has been closed due to inclement weather. You can even tweet the word of the day from Merriam-Webster's to help build students' vocabulary! Twitter also allows you to follow and re-tweet educational information from other academic organizations, as well as educational blogs and new articles.

Before you go tweeting out into the world, however, make sure to protect your tweets so they're visible only to those you approve. (Go under "Settings" and choose "Security and Privacy" to protect your tweets.) This protects not only your privacy, but also that of your students.

Twitter has some great features that can prove useful in education, such as the hashtag (#). You've seen the hashtag watermark on the screen during your favorite television shows, but what exactly does it mean? The hashtag allows users to join in a conversation specific to that particular key word. For example, let's say you want to spread the word that your school needs volunteers for the annual holiday school dance. Simply compose a tweet that includes the hashtag in front of any key word or phrase (no spaces if there are

multiple words), like: "Looking for parent volunteers for our annual event #PS101HolidayDance." By clicking on the hyperlinked hashtag, parents can sign up to volunteer and can even post additional questions, comments, or even pictures. Anyone who clicks on the hyperlink hashtag will see a history of the conversation, including who offered their services, who wants to be on the setup committee or cleanup crew, who can chaperone, who can bring snacks or drinks, and so on. Using the hashtag in Twitter allows for a collaborative effort when it comes to school functions in a very efficient, real-time mobile way.

Here are other ways you can incorporate Twitter into your classroom:

1. Study Groups

Students in the upper grades can use Twitter to form study groups (with parents' and administrators' permissions, of course). Students can ask and answer pertinent questions on a variety of topics that they are studying. You can even bring in multiple teachers from different areas of the curriculum to collaborate with students in a way unlike any other!

2. Instant Survey

Use the hashtag feature in Twitter to gather instant feedback from your followers in a survey-style approach and create discussion topics in one convenient, streamlined feed to parents (and perhaps teachers as well). Compose a tweet with a particular question in mind, such as:

✿ "Help us help you: What are some areas our school should work on? #PS3SuggestionBox"

✿ "What types of books does your child like to read? #MrHymanClassFavoriteBooks"

✿ "Have you visited our school website lately? Tell us what you think. #PS41SchoolWebsite"

3. Virtual Planning Sessions or Professional Development Meetings

Set up a hashtag feed on Twitter and start your planning or professional development discussion with other teachers while waiting for a faculty meeting to start or even while waiting in line at the supermarket or at the bank. As an alternative, you could also click on the "Discover #" button on your mobile device's Twitter app and enter "professionaldevelopment" (no space) in the search box at the top of the screen. Click "Search" to discover professional-development opportunities and conversations on a worldwide scale.

Using Pinterest to Showcase and Share Ideas

Have you ever wanted to share educational ideas in a picture format instead of having to describe an idea? What if you could do both? That's the idea behind Pinterest, an online content-sharing tool that allows users to "pin" images, articles, videos, and much more on virtual boards, which can be public or private.

Organizing "pins" on an online board opens up a wide array of uses for teachers and administrators everywhere. For example, utilize Pinterest to organize a class wish list pictorially. Create a board, name it "Our Class Wish List," and post pictures of the supplies you so desperately need. E-mail the link to your class parents (or entire school if you can), tweet out the information, and post a link on your school website, and you may get the art supplies for an upcoming project with your students or even that fancy all-in-one color copier.

You can also use Pinterest to build an online portfolio of great teaching ideas—yours and those of other educators—to use in the classroom or enhance your own professional development. It's a great way to organize those teacher shortcuts, technology-incorporation ideas, classroom management ideas, projects, or lesson ideas in one convenient place. See an example by visiting my boards (http://pinterest.com/ps101hyman/adam-hyman/) to see how Pinterest can help you in your teaching!

Broadcasting School Events

UStream.tv is a free web-based Internet service that allows members to broadcast their own programming to an online audience. Users can create private, password-protected channels so that the content being broadcast is seen only by those for whom it is intended.

Why might you use UStream.tv for your school? UStream.tv not only allows for an online audience (your school community), it also enables you to record and stream special events live, such as a school play, an awards ceremony, a special assembly, or the principal's weekly message for the school. Parents can watch the events either live or on demand from the comfort of their own homes or workplaces.

In my school, for example, we started to broadcast (and record) some of our monthly Parents' Association meetings because there were too many conflicting schedules with our parent body. Some parents might work late, take their child to soccer practice, or just have prior appointments. It was becoming increasingly difficult to get the attendance that we needed. So we broadcast the meetings to reach those parents who couldn't physically be at the meeting, effectively communicating to a much larger percentage of parents overall. The result was astonishing! Sometimes we had more parents physically in attendance, and sometimes we had more parents watching it live from home. But we always had more parents view the meetings in the days that followed a recorded meeting—especially when we advertised a reminder through an email blast or on the school's website. Ultimately, this allowed us to reach a parent audience that numbered in the hundreds of views, versus the 20 to 30 parents that were able to show up.

The use of technology and UStream.tv allows for a broader reach when it comes to communication between a school and the community it serves. Now, instead of just hearing secondhand what took place at a meeting or an event, parents can log on to the school's UStream.tv channel and see for themselves. It truly brings everyone together in ways that just weren't possible in the past!

QUICK TECH TIP

Be sure to have appropriate picture and video release forms from all the students and teachers in your school if you plan to have them appear online.

A Growing Concern for Cyberbullying

One item that has been a hot topic in recent years is cyberbullying. What makes cyberbullying so dangerous is that it can occur at any time and in multiple ways. Cyberbullying situations don't necessarily occur in the classroom, schoolyard, or lunchroom. Cyberbullying doesn't have in-person, face-to-face situations. Cyberbullying takes place online and can consist of harassing or threatening text messages, email messages, social media posts, and even chats. It's a relatively easy way for students to pick on others with harsh words and can lead to huge problems.

If you are going to utilize any of the online resources or social media tools that have been mentioned here, it's important to take a few essential precautions to make sure that students, teachers, and parents understand that cyberbullying is very serious and can have major consequences for anyone involved.

Prior to introducing online tools and resources to students, take the time to send out information and guidelines to parents. You may even choose to conduct a parent/student workshop in advance of, or in conjunction with, the introduction of certain online tools. Both parents and students should know and be aware that the use of these powerful learning tools is a privilege and that they need to follow specific guidelines set forth by you and the school. Always spell out the rules and regulations with proper online etiquette, and always lay out the consequences in a clear and meaningful way. For example, when I introduced the use of Google Drive and Gmail accounts, I established the rule that students must invite not only their classmates and teachers into their online collaborations, but also at least one parent or guardian. This addresses two issues: First and foremost, parents can be actively involved with their child's education by seeing the work they are doing online. Secondly, involving adults tends to take cyberbullying out of the equation. Now, will you have students who will test to see how far they can push the envelope? Unfortunately, yes. However, inviting parents and guardians into their child's work dramatically deters students and keeps incidents to a minimum.

With Common Core State Standards in place, students should be exposed to online collaboration and social media for the purpose of college and career readiness, but they should also take seriously the responsibilities that come with using such tools. The more teachers and parents stress appropriate behavior and responsibility, the more students will respect the power that they have in their hands to use these tools in an appropriate and sensitive manner.

Bibliography

CDG-W. (June 26, 2012). "2012 learn now, lecture later report." In *CDW Newsroom.* Retrieved November 15, 2013, from http://www.cdwnewsroom. com/2012-learn-now-lecture-later-report/.

Macpherson, E. (March 4, 2013). "Edubrawl: Where real life teachers talk tech." In *We Are Teachers.* Retrieved November 15, 2013, from http:// www.weareteachers.com/community/blogs/weareteachersblog/blog-wat/2013/03/04/edubrawl-where-real-life-teachers-talk-tech.

National Governors Association Center for Best Practices & Council of Chief State School Officers. (2010). *Common core state standards (English language arts standards).* Washington, DC: National Governors Association Center for Best Practices, Council of Chief State School Officers.

Purcell, K., Rainie, L., Heaps, A., Buchanan, J., Friedrich, L., Jacklin, A., Chen, C. & Zickuhr, K. (November 1, 2012). "How teens do research in the digital world." In Pew Internet. Retrieved November 15, 2013, from http://pewinternet.org/ Reports/2012/Student-Research.aspx.

Swan, K., Schenker, J. & Kratcoski, A. (2008). "The effects of the use of interactive whiteboards on student achievement." In J. Luca & E. Weippl (Eds.), *Proceedings of world conference on educational multimedia, hypermedia and telecommunications 2008* (pp. 3290-3297). Chesapeake, VA: AACE. Retrieved November 15, 2013, from http://www.editlib.org/p/28842.

Additional Resources:

Dunn, J. (October 24, 2011). "The teacher's guide to keeping students safe online." In *Edudemic.* Retrieved November 15, 2013, from http://www. edudemic.com/student-online-safety-guide/.

Dunn, J. (October 4, 2013). "The biggest edtech trends: What teachers really think." In *Edudemic.* Retrieved November 15, 2013, from http://www.edudemic. com/edtech-trends-teachers/.

Hertz, M.B. (July 10, 2012). "The flipped classroom: Pro and con." In *edutopia*. Retrieved November 15, 2013, from http://www.edutopia.org/blog/flipped-classroom-pro-and-con-mary-beth-hertz.

Hill, S. (November 24, 2012). "How tablets are invading the classroom." In *Digital Trends*. Retrieved November 15, 2013, from http://www.digitaltrends.com/mobile/tablets-invading-the-classroom/.

Madan, V. (May 16, 2011). "6 reasons tablets are ready for the classroom." In *Mashable*. Retrieved November 15, 2013, from http://mashable.com/2011/05/16/tablets-education/.

TabletsforSchools. (July 29, 2013). "10 big concerns about tablets in the classroom." In *Edudemic*. Retrieved November 15, 2013, from http://www.edudemic.com/10-big-concerns-about-tablets-in-the-classroom/.

Wilson, L. & Gileniak, M. (2011). *Technology for learning: A guidebook for change*. Retrieved November 15, 2013, from http://reg.accelacomm.com/servlet/Frs.FrsGetContent?id=40147540.

Recommended Websites:

Education – YouTube
http://www.youtube.com/education

Ezvid
http://www.ezvid.com

Flipped Learning Network
http://www.flippedlearning.org/FLN

Google Drive
http://drive.google.com

ooVoo
http://www.oovoo.com

Pinterest
http://www.pinterest.com

Pinterest–Adam Hyman
http://www.pinterest.com/ps101hyman/adam-hyman

Prezi
http://prezi.com

Screenr
http://www.screenr.com

Skype in the Classroom
http://education.skype.com

SMART Exchange
http://exchange.smarttech.com

SMART Notebook Express
http://express.smarttech.com

SMART Technologies
http://smarttech.com

StopBullying.gov
http://www.stopbullying.gov/cyberbullying/

TeacherTube
http://www.teachertube.com

Twitter
http://twitter.com

UStream
http://www.ustream.tv

Yahoo Web Hosting
http://smallbusiness.yahoo.com/webhosting

Notes